Sussex
Coast Road
Richard Powell

Published in 2024 by

U P Publications, St George's House, George St,
Huntingdon, Cambridgeshire, PE29 3GH. UK
+44 208 133 0123   manager@uppublications.ltd.uk

© 2023 Richard Powell

Richard Powell has asserted his moral rights
under the Copyright, Designs & Patents Act 1988,
to be identified as the Author of this Work

All Rights Reserved - No part of this publication may be
reproduced or transmitted by any means, electronic,
mechanical, photocopy or otherwise, without the prior
permission of the author or publisher except for the
purpose of research or editorial use. This is a work of
non-fiction based on the information available at the
time of publication and the author's experience in the field.
Image credits and copyrights are listed at the back of the
book. A catalogue record for this book is available from the
British Library. Licensed Fonts: Caviar Dreams, Concept.

ISBN 13: 978-1-912777-53-2

www.uppbooks.com

1. Detail from a Postcard Map of Sussex

Introduction
by Richard Powell

2. Camber Sands Beach

A tour of the Sussex Coast takes us through some of the most fascinating towns and beautiful countryside in England. This book is more than just a tourist guide, it contains anecdotes, pictures, strange facts and oddities known to the locals. From Rye to Chichester, we find bustling modern cities, historic tourist towns and ancient villages, cliffs with sweeping views of the channel, sand dune lined beaches, rolling hills, great houses and gardens, castles and history going back over thousands of years. We experience exciting nightlife, great food, exotic hotels, quiet country lanes, historic pubs, modern shopping malls and unique stores. Come with us and enjoy the sights, people and places of the southeast coast of England.

The A259 follows the coast from Folkestone in Kent to just short of Portsmouth in Hampshire. This book covers the route from Rye to Chichester Harbour in Sussex. Most of the 90 miles covered consists of a single carriageway that tends to follow the coast with a few twists and turns inland. If you are driving, please be careful, it is busy and often narrow and is considered to be one of the more dangerous roads in England.

Most of these places are less than two hours away by train from London. Driving can take about the same time but we were sometimes caught in heavy traffic. Stopping to look around became a pleasure. Starting from the east, the first of these English Channel coastal stops is the town of Rye. First though, let's go down to the beach of Camber Sands. Behind these dunes is the village of Camber, our first stop.

3. *A view of boats moored on the River Rother in the town of Rye, Sussex*

Chapter One
Camber to Rye Harbour

Camber

Camber is a small village behind the dunes of the River Rother two miles from Rye. Until the late 19th century, it consisted of a few fishermen's shacks. Now it is a very popular vacation spot with several large holiday parks, restaurants and shops that cater to the visitors.

Its popularity grew in the 1890s when tourists started to visit Rye and some residents decided that they needed a golf course. This was built on the dunes between the village and the river. By 1905, it had over 430 members including 60 ladies, mostly from London. Before the age of the motor car, getting down to the beach and the links with your equipment was a bit of a chore. So, in 1895, the 1 ¾ mile Rye and Camber tramway was opened with a steam engine. It eventually lost the battle against the automobile and was closed after the Admiralty used it in WWII.

4. Rye and Camber Tramway - 'Victoria' with train crosses Broadwater Bridge (1914)

5. Camber Sands

Camber Sands

Camber Sands is the only significant sandy beach in Sussex and the only major sand dune system. The beach on the east side of the River Rother stretches nearly three miles to Kent. It can be very busy in the summer, but at other times of the year, we can have long peaceful strolls and find only the occasional dog walker.

The sand dunes behind the beach are so extensive that they have been used in movies, including one where it was represented as the Sahara Desert. At one point filming was delayed due to snow.

The area looks so much like the Normandy beaches that the military practised landings here for D-Day. Parts of the movie, The Longest Day, were filmed here too. The whole area was heavily fortified during WWII.

Because of the shifting sands, the beach and dunes are still growing. The dunes have been designated a 'Site of Special Scientific Interest' and a 'Site of Nature Conservation Importance'. The beach is worth a visit especially in the summer as it is unique to England.

Rye

Rye is one of those places that just drips with history and sights to see. Here, we find tales of smugglers and shipwrecks, writers and wars. In the centre of the old village, narrow cobbled Mermaid Street is one of the most photographed views in Sussex. We were enthralled by the quaintness of the scene which really looks like old England. From here we can see timbered buildings housing pubs, stores and homes.

One of the most famous inns in the UK is on Mermaid Street and of course, it is named the Mermaid Inn. Built in the 12th century, the cellars are the only part left that is that old. What we see now was mostly built in the 15th and 16th centuries.

Smuggling was big business in the 18th century and the notorious Hawkhurst Gang hung out at the Mermaid Inn. This infamous gang operated all along the channel coast for over 10 years with almost complete impunity. Supposedly, tunnels in the cellars of the Mermaid lead to other nearby inns and were used for quick escapes and hiding their booty. It finally took the militia to beat this cruel and bloodthirsty gang in battle in 1747.

In its current manifestation, the inn offers an excellently decorated bar and restaurant and an absolutely unique hotel.

6. *Mermaid Street, Rye*

7. Mermaid Inn

Reported to be one of the most haunted places in Britain, each of the 31 rooms has a different theme. On offer are rooms with four poster beds and low ceiling rafters, hidden passageways, a sliding bookcase and priest bolt holes. We can enjoy a night, and maybe some sleep, in a piece of English history.

For the energetic, climbing to the top of the tower of the 800-year-old St. Mary's church provides great views over the roofs and streets. On a clear day, we can see the harbour and miles down the channel coast. Rye's museum is in the Ypres tower. This 600-year-old fort was built into the town walls as defence against the French. It has seen life as a prison, soup kitchen and a mortuary.

We had to stop and see historic Lamb House. Owned by the National Trust since 1950 the house was built by local wine merchant, James Lamb, in 1722. Legend has it that four years later King George I took shelter here one night when his ship was stuck on the nearby sands. He was lucky to be there, as his wife had a baby that night.

The house has attracted great writers including Henry James, E.F. Benson and more recently Joan Aikens.

Sussex Coast Road 9

8. Ypres Tower Museum

Both James and Benson complained about the house's poltergeist. The building and its walled garden is a lovely peaceful spot to enjoy a sunny day. Benson's novels about the town and the house, Mapp and Lucia, were filmed here in 2014 by the BBC. We saw some of Henry James's personal possessions on display.

Walking through the old town, we explored antique shops, including a kitchen shop where my grandmother would recognize most of the wares on sale. On Wednesday mornings a farmers market attracts crowds outside the Cinque Ports pub. The former Beatle, Paul McCartney has made Rye home for many years.

Rye Harbour

A short detour to Rye Harbour is well worth the time. We exit Rye heading west on the A259 and cross the bridge over the River Bede. About half a mile along, we turn left crossing the river again on Harbour Road. The right turn heads us toward Camber Castle. When built, in 1512, by Henry VII, the castle was close to the sea and protected the Rye anchorage from French attack. It quickly became useless as the harbour silted up and France and England were at peace. Currently owned by Heritage England, this Grade I Listed building is deserving of exploring.

9. Camber Castle

One advantage of having the harbour silt up was it created a wonderful place for wildlife. For a little peace, we wandered around the Rye Harbour Conservation Area. The paths take us through the marshes which are home to hundreds of rare and endangered species of birds, animals and plants. Tragedy struck here in 1928 when the 17-man crew of the RNLI lifeboat Mary Stanford drowned while trying to reach a boat in distress. The abandoned lifeboat station has been left here on the beach in memory to the men who died. There is a large memorial beside the Church of the Holy Spirit.

There is a lot more to see in Rye but now we are continuing on. Heading back the way we came, we reach the A259 again and turn left (west) towards our next stop.

10. Rye Marshes

11. *St Thomas the Martyr church and village cross, Winchelsea*

Chapter Two
Winchelsea to Hastings

Stane Streeet Looking South

12. Winchelsea, St Thomas, Window

Winchelsea

About two miles down the A259 from Rye is the little seaside town of Winchelsea. The original town was destroyed by sea erosion and floods in the 1200s. At its peak, it boasted six thousand inhabitants due mainly to trade with Europe, wool exports and wine imports. In 1288, King Edward I ordered the new town to be rebuilt on a grid layout. The town was destroyed by French and Spanish invaders, suffered the black death and then had the cliffs eroded and finally, the shore shifted leaving Winchelsea without a harbour. No luck at all.

We stopped in the town centre to see the church of St. Thomas the Martyr, named for Thomas Becket who was murdered in Canterbury Cathedral in 1170. Part of the church is in ruins due to one of the French invasions, but a large part was beautifully restored in Victorian times. There are five effigies under beautifully carved canopies. The graveyard is large and contains the 2002 grave of Spike Mulligan.

A couple of miles southwest on the A259 brings us to the ancient village of Icklesham. About halfway between Rye and Icklesham is a cute little tea shop where all sorts of produce can be purchased. A lovely distraction. We spotted the windmill at the top of Hogs Hill. This was used by Paul McCartney as a recording studio. Another few miles through picturesque farmland gets us to our next destination.

15. Walk over Pett Level with Hog Hill in the background

14. St. Thomas the Martyr

Hastings

Although the Normans landed at Pevensey, down the coast to the west, and the battle took place 8 miles northeast of the town, Hastings is known in history for the battle where Willian conquered England in 1066.

When the A259 reaches the sea in Hastings, turning left we find the Rock-a-Nore area. The shingle beach here is called the Stade, Saxon for "landing place". For hundreds of years, and still in operation today, is the beach launched fishing fleet, purported to be the largest in Europe. Because of the unstable seabed here, any attempt to build a harbour has met with failure. The groynes were built in the 1800s to keep the beach from moving. It worked so well that the beach has actually grown larger and created room for more fish boats.

The distinctive tall black wooden structures along the beach are fishnet huts.

Contrary to popular belief, they are not used to dry hanging fishnets. That is done in the sun on the beach. These buildings are used for net storage. They were built multi-storey because there originally was not enough room on the beach. Black tar was used to seal the buildings from the weather. The fishermen's museum tells us all about it.

15. *Fishing Boats on East Beach*

16. *Stade Beach Fisherman's Dinghy*

17. *Fishermen's Huts*

Across the road, we have one of Hastings' two funicular railways. The East Hill Lift, opened in 1902, has the steepest gradient in England at 38 degrees. It is now run by electricity, but until the 1970s it used water as a counterbalance to move the cars up and down. The car at the top filled its 600-gallon tank while the one at the bottom was emptied. The heavier car at the top pulled the bottom one back up where the procedure was repeated. At the top, we find East Hill Park where we get great views of the town and beach. For the lovers of funicular railways, you can duplicate the experience further along at West Hill.

At the base station of the East Hill railway is a peculiar conical shaped structure with a sign that reads 'waste not want not'. The natural spring here is called East Well and the water can be accessed from a tap. In 1846 a fire destroyed some of the fishermen's net sheds. Money was raised to replace them and there was some cash left over. So in 1848 Dr. McCabe raised more money and built a 1,500 gallon reservoir for public use. There is a story that a fisherman used the well as his legal address when signing documents.

Most of the old town was built in the 19th century and the narrow streets and character buildings and shops give the place a lovely Victorian feel. We spent hours wandering around the warren of

18. *East Hill funicular railway station*

19. *East Hill Well*

Sussex Coast Road   19

20. *East Hill funicular railway station*

streets filled with great antique stores, galleries, second hand shops, and some pretty "olde worlde" pubs and restaurants. Hastings was used as the backdrop for the British TV series called Foyle's War, a perfect setting for the 1940s. One last thing that gives this town the old Victorian tourist feel is the promenade. On one side is the channel and on the other are the terraced houses built by the rich and famous of the time. Most look well maintained but the old summer homes have been converted into flats, small hotels, B&Bs or restaurants.

Further west, we can look up and see the ruins of the castle built by William the Conqueror. By taking Hastings' second funicular railway we get up to the castle and West hill. Over its 900-year history, the castle has not had much luck. William ordered the building of a wooden castle even before the battle. Two years later he ordered it be rebuilt in stone. It changed hands a few times until 1287 when storms caused the cliffs to collapse taking part of the castle with it. Over the next hundred years, it was attacked and burned by the French twice and more of it

21. The view from the East Hill funicular railway

crumbled as the cliffs continued to deteriorate. By the end of the 16th century, it was overgrown and mostly forgotten until 1824 when it was dug out and partially restored. To add further insult, it was bombed by the Germans in WWII.

Today it is a great place to explore and enjoy the views of the coast around Hastings.

23. *Hastings Castle*

24. *Hastings Beach front with Hastings Castle on the hill, behind*

Sussex Coast Road

25. Hastings Seafront 1934

The Pier, Hastings

Hastings Pier has unique history with many high points and as well as many lows. It has seen fires, storms and unstable supports. On the good side, it has been saved from destruction several times, has seen crowds coming for great entertainment and been awarded prizes for design.

Here are some of its stories over the last 150 years.

It was designed by Eugenius Birch, who also designed Brighton and Eastbourne piers, and officially opened in 1872. It was immediately very popular with the tourists. The ballroom at the end of the pier which could accommodate 2,000 people, was destroyed by fire in 1917. The safe was located by the pier's diver 3 days later, completely intact. Several other offices were also lost including all the local fishing club's angling equipment and the costumes for the Aristocrats, the pier's resident troupe. It took five years to replace it.

The 1930s turned out to be the heydays for the pier, attracting London day trippers, holiday makers and locals. Additional buildings including a theatre were added with the popular Art Deco designs. The pavilion at the end of the pier was rebuilt to include a ballroom, a bar and a cafe. Open-air terraces on the first floor provided the visitors with great views of the channel and

26. *Hastings Pier with 1966 Embroidery Exhibition Pavilion*

27. Hastings Old Pier

the town of Hastings. WWII put an abrupt end to this as the pier was closed for fear that the invading Germans would use it as part of their landing. Some of the planking was removed to impede any invaders. After the war, it returned to the popularity of the 30s.

Through the 1960s and 70s, the pavilion became a major player in contemporary rock music history. It hosted Welsh crooner Tom Jones, guitar legend Jimi Hendrix, rock bands The Rolling Stones, The Who, Genesis, Ten Years After, Motorhead, Status Quo and Pink Floyd.

1966 was the 900th anniversary of the Battle of Hastings. The 'Hastings Embroidery' was commissioned to show 81 separate scenes in British history. To exhibit this 243-foot tapestry, the bandstand was replaced by a circular white dome called the Triodome. Later this dome housed a zoo and then an amusement arcade. In 1986 it was dismantled and sold for scrap. Later that year, it turned up at the end of Brighton Palace Pier.

Real problems began in 1990 when a severe storm did a million pounds of damage and weakened the structure. Over the next 15 years, it changed owners several times and finally in 2006 it was closed by the council after finding that the supports were unstable. With £300,000 in repairs, it opened again in 2007 only to be partially closed again the next year. The locals formed a trust to save the pier and a "Save the Pier" march was held in October of 2009. Disaster struck again, a year later, where suspected arson destroyed most of the wooden superstructure.

Over the next few years, with funds from the council, the trust, Heritage England and the Lottery, the support structure was repaired and the deck reconstructed. It was reopened to the public in 2016. In 2017 it won the "Pier of the Year" award and the Stirling architecture award. Due to ownership problems, it has been opened and closed on numerous occasions. As of April 2021 the pier is open, once again attracting crowds enjoying a day at the sea.

28. St Leonards on Sea Beach Front

Chapter Three
St. Leonards to Bexhill

St. Leonards-On-Sea

Travel a little way down the A259 west along the Hastings seafront and without noticing we are now in St. Leonards, a purpose-built beach resort town for the wealthy in the 1820s. Originally two separate towns, St. Leonards and Hastings amalgamated in the late 19th century. A London property developer, James Burton, purchased the land which had been part of a farm. Unlike the cliffs at Hastings, this land slopes down to the sea. He built a new village with villas, seafront houses, hotels, shops, services, parks and a turnpike to the town. He also built an archway to mark the boundary with Hastings.

The town quickly became very fashionable and attracted royalty including the future queen, Princess Victoria and her mother. Because it was so popular, it started expanding eastward along the seafront. Not to be outdone, Hastings started building west toward St. Leonards. In the 1870s there were 3 miles of built-up seafront with no vacant land between the two towns. In 1875 they merged to become the County Brough of Hastings. Fifty years from farmland to a luxury seafront resort.

There is one building that we could not help but notice right on the waterfront, the Marine Court. Opened in 1937, the Art-Deco apartment and commercial complex resembles a cruise ship.

29. St. Leonards-on-Sea Pier

30. Marine Court

Sussex Coast Road 29

It is now a listed building and the locals are restoring it.

Like most seaside resorts, St. Leonards had a pier. Opened in 1891 it proved very popular with a pavilion and a dance hall. Unfortunately, WWII put paid to the pier. Like most of the others on this coast, it was cut in half because of the fears of a German invasion. It was not rebuilt.

Just a quick note here before we continue. For the history buffs, a quick trip to the village of Battle may be of interest.

It is only 10 miles up the road from Hastings. Here we can look out over the field in which William the Conqueror from Normandy defeated the English king, Harold, in the year 1066. This battle defined the next 950 years of world history. Battle Abby was built by the Normans as penance for killing so many people in his conquering of England. The ruins are worth the time to explore.

31. Battlefield and Abbey

Bexhill

Back on the A259, on the road to Bexhill is a field where different festivals, circuses and entertainments are held. Known as Glyne Gap, it has a spooky reputation. On some days the morning mists do not clear here until much later in the day and it is unusually quiet. Some years ago, a man walking to work early one morning is reported to have seen a ghostly army marching up the gap and disappearing into the fog.

Many battles have been fought along this piece of coast. Roman soldiers marched through here 2,000 years ago. Saxon King Offa defeated the men of the Hastings tribe in 771. Vikings pillaged the countryside for hundreds of years. The battle of Hastings was fought not 10 miles away. The French raided the coast continually in the Middle Ages. Smuggling here was considered a career occupation. In WWII this area was protected by thousands of Canadian soldiers to keep the Germans from invading. On a direct route to London, many German bombs were dropped along this valley. Some things, whatever they are, do not like to leave.

On to Bexhill where we find another purpose build beach resort town for the rich, built in the late 1800s.

The history of the town goes back to the 8th century when Saxon King Offa built a church. Mostly destroyed during the Norman conquest, the area was given to one of William's faithful knights. It changed hands a few times before, in 1561, Queen Elizabeth I gave it to Thomas Sackville whose descendants owned it for the next 400 years. One of its biggest claims to fame is that England's first ever motor car races were held here in 1902.

One outstanding building that cannot be missed in Bexhill is the De La Warr Pavilion. Opened in 1935, this modernistic public building contained a theatre, restaurant, reading room and lounge. The military took it over during WWII and it fell into disrepair. It finally became a listed building in 1986 and funds were found to return it to its former glory. Reopened in 2005, the unique shaped building now acts as a very popular art gallery and cultural centre.

As with many of these tourist towns built along the southeast coast, the town has a lovely row of terraced seaside houses built along the promenade. Many of these have been converted to small hotels, B&Bs, and restaurants. Bexhill also has a lovely 'Old Town' with many large Victorian homes and the ruins of the old manor house and gardens. There is a tale that the smells of home cooking that would have come from these houses 150

33. *De La Warr Pavilion*

years ago, fill the air with no visible source. Hungry visitors cannot find the restaurants that are serving this delicious smelling food.

Follow the A259 from Bexhill old town west for a couple of miles and we leave the built-up area and into farmland. The road here is about a mile inland from the channel as we head to Pevensey Bay.

34. Bexhill Seafront Mansions

35. *Aerial view of Bexhill*

36. *Pevensey Bay*

Chapter Four
Pevensey to Eastbourne

Pevensey

At the roundabout, we take the A259 exit which leads to the town of Pevensey. The A259 makes a left turn at the first road and heads toward Pevensey Bay. Do not turn yet, as we need to explore the town itself. Stay straight on the High Street and stop for a look at the old castle. The topography has changed a lot since William the Conqueror landed his fleet in 1066. The spit of land has eroded and now the beach is all pebbles barely above sea level.

When first constructed in the 3rd century, the sea came up to the stone walls, providing a strong defensive position. Of the twelve forts built by the Romans, along the coast, this is the only one that has survived. We are not sure who the enemy was, because, at that time, the local Romans rebelled and in 296AD Rome had to reconquer England. After the Romans left, the community was sheltered here until 471AD, when Saxon raiders captured it and slaughtered everyone.

The Anglo Saxons did come back, but not for a while. On the morning of September 28, 1066, the locals could have watched from the walls as William's 700 ships landed in the bay facing the fort.

In 1067 after the success of the battle of Hastings, William gave it to his half-brother Robert who subsequently re-enforced the old Roman walls and built a castle

37. Aerial view of Pevensey Castle

38. Archery Tavern c 1925

within the old fort. As the bay was a natural harbour facing Normandy, William wanted to keep it safe. Over the following centuries, it has been ruined and repaired many times. It was even used as a prison for James I of Scotland. In 1925 the owner, the Duke of Devonshire, gave it to the government who again repaired it as an historic monument. This is, more or less, what we see today. The last bit of the castle's history involved being set up as a defensive position against a German invasion. Nearly 1,700 years of fascinating history all in one spot.

Back to the road and we drive the half mile to the lovely small beach resort of Pevensey Bay. It has a long shingle beach with most of the facilities of the other larger beach towns along the coast. Of historic interest are the two Martello Towers built in the early 1800s as a defence against a Napoleonic invasion.

The area between Pevensey Bay and Eastbourne is known as the Crumbles. During the 1920s it was the scene of two separate murders of young women. The first was 17-year-old Irene Munro in 1920. On holiday alone she was befriended by two young men at the Archery Tavern.

They beat her to death with a brick then buried her body near the beach leaving a foot sticking out.

A 13-year-old boy almost tripped over it. Witnesses testified in court that they had seen the two men with Irene. They were found guilty and hanged.

The second murder was of 38-year-old Emily Kaye. She was killed by her lover Patrick Mahon in 1924 who had convinced her that they should marry and emigrate to South Africa. She withdrew over £400 and gave it to Patrick. She did not know that he was already married. In the cottage they had rented near the beach, Patrick killed Emily and proceeded to dismember and burn her body. Pieces of the pulverised bones were spread around the garden.

With the help of his wife, the police found enough evidence to have him convicted of Emily's murder.

He too was hanged.

Driving again on the A259 out of Pevensey Bay, we pass through some farmland and past a golf course and in a mile and a half we come to the first roundabout of Eastbourne.

39. Aerial photo of Sovereign harbour in Eastbourne along the entrance and the start of Pevensey bay.

Eastbourne

Going south, toward the sea, either of these roundabouts will take us to the man-made Sovereign Marina. Opened in 1993, it is now one of the biggest marinas in all of Europe. It has all the facilities of a modern marina including fuel docks, boat repair, chandlers, private yacht and fish boat berthing. Around the marina, various types of housing developments have been built, plus commercial enterprises including a shopping centre and restaurants. The entrance to the harbour is marked by another of the Martello towers. This project has added much to the growth of Eastbourne in the last 25 years which now has a population of over 100,000.

Human habitation of the area goes back to before the Celts in 500 BC. The quiet fishing village of Eastbourne became a seaside resort when in the summer of 1780, King George III's children stayed here to enjoy the health benefits of the sea. It was not until the mid-1800s that the Duke of Devonshire developed the seaside town. By 1890 the population had jumped from 4,000 to 35,000. WWII was devastating for the town as it was continually raided by German Bombers. After the war and until the present day, Eastbourne has grown continually as a holiday resort and a commercial centre.

The Neo-Grecian bandstand with its blue dome is unique to the UK.

40. Eastbourne Pier and Bandstand

41. Aerial view of Eastbourne

When opened in 1935, the semi-circular structure could hold 3,500 people on the main floor and two balconies. Due to health and safety, the number of attendees has been cut to 1,600. For many years, military bands would play most days from spring till the end of October. Over the years the attendance started to drop and the performances were cut back. In 2001 to save the bandstand and bring in new audiences, they put on rock and roll and swing concerts. This was extended to include the 'Last Night of the Proms' and the '1812 Overture' with fireworks. Attending a performance is a bit of what it was like for our grandparents' holiday at the sea. There is a blue plaque here for local bandsman John Wesley Woodward who performed on the Titanic as it sank in 1912.

Another popular historic site is the Redoubt Fortress and Museum. Built over 200 years ago to protect England from a Napoleonic invasion, the circular moated fort was used as late as WWII to protect the country from a German invasion. Now, fully restored, it houses the military collections from 3 separate regiments plus displays from the current armed forces.

For the art lover, a visit to the Towner Art Gallery is a must. Upon his death in 1920, Alderman John Towner bequeathed the town 22 paintings and £6,000 to start an art gallery. Opened in 1923, the art gallery was located in an 18th century manor house in the Old Town. The gallery grew slowly with donations from major artists and with temporary exhibitions.

42. *Eastbourne Redoubt*

With the sale of the manor house, the gallery was closed in 2005. A new building was opened in 2009. Its architecture is designed to reflect the South Downs which rise up behind Eastbourne. The Towner Art Gallery has been described as the largest gallery in the south of England.

Eastbourne is a gentler, more sophisticated version of Brighton. The pier is still a big attraction, but like many of the wooden south coast piers, it has suffered fire damage but has been reopened. The Victorian period houses along the 3 miles of seafront have been well maintained and keep the air of a classic seaside resort. The highlight of the promenade is the beautiful floral display called the Carpet Gardens. Flowers from around the world bloom here adding to the town's popularity. The old town shopping area in Eastbourne, called Little Chelsea, has been named one of the 'coolest' places in England. It is full of boutiques, antique shops, crafts stores and eateries. Eastbourne used to be called 'God's waiting room' because of the number of older people retiring there. That has changed with the average age dropping below 45. It now has industries employing thousands and many London commuters looking for a lovely affordable place to live.

43. *Carpet Gardens, Grand Parade, Eastbourne*

Sussex Coast Road

44. Low tide at Beachy Head

Chapter Five
Beachy Head to Exceat

Beachy Head

One of Eastbourne's biggest attractions is not in the town but a few miles further west. From the pier, we follow the King Edward Parade (B2103) along the coast. This drive passes lovely terraced houses on the right and the beach on our left. Stay on the B2103 out of Eastbourne. The road becomes Upper Dicker Road and then Beachy Head Road. Near the top of the hill turning left gets us to our next destination.

There is no beach at Beachy Head. But we find one of the highest chalk cliffs in England rising to over 530 feet. The name is a corruption of the French name beau chef meaning beautiful headland. On a clear day, we can see the Isle of Wight over 50 miles away. Years ago, Eastbourne Council bought 4,000 acres of land surrounding the cliff to prevent development. The cliff itself is continually being eroded and minor collapses happen regularly. Large collapses occur very infrequently, usually after heavy rains and them freezing temperatures.

Beachy Head has appeared in dozens of movies and TV shows including The Who's 1979 classic Quadrophenia, where in the final scene, we see the Vespa scooter going over the cliff. The pub and restaurant near the top offer a peaceful place for a meal or drink while we enjoy the view.

It has been reported as the 3rd

45. Beachy Head Lighthouse

most popular suicide location in the world. Every year 20 or more people jump from the cliff to their deaths. Suicides here have been recorded as early as the 7th century. Today, to help cut down on these deaths, the area is patrolled by a Chaplaincy Team and there is a phone box nearby with the number for the Samaritans. We did not wander too close to the edge as there have been stories about the ghost of the black monk who encourages visitors to come a bit closer.

At the Beachy Head Story exhibition, we discovered how the cliffs were formed and the tales of people who have lived there for centuries. The helpful staff at this family-friendly attraction gave us ideas of what to see and which trails to hike.

Seven Sisters

To the west, the chalk cliff hills and the valleys between them are named the Seven Sisters. They run from Beachy Head to the town of Seaford. They are the ends of the Downs where they meet the sea. These cliffs are one of the most photographed places in England, often mistaken for the white cliffs of Dover.

They are whiter and have less development which makes them

46. Looking over Cuckmere Haven and the Seven Sisters white chalk cliffs

47. Belle Tout Lighthouse

more attractive. They have been used in many movies including Braveheart.

Here we follow the Beachy Head Road rather than the A259 which here is about a mile inland. This road takes us near the cliffs and, in a mile, we come upon one of the most famous lighthouses in Britain, Belle Tout.

The original wooden one was built in 1828 and the present stone one was completed in 1832.

It was not as successful as hoped because of cliff erosion and heavy fog which blocked the sight of the light. It was closed in 1902 when the Beachy Head Lighthouse was built at sea level below the cliff at Beachy Head.

Belle Tout changed hands a few times after that. In WWII it was accidentally badly damaged by Canadian Artillery during a practice session.

The council bought it because of its historical significance and it was restored in 1956. In the 1980s, BBC used it for a TV mini-series. It was also used in a James Bond movie. The most amazing thing about this structure was that in 1999 the complete lighthouse was moved in one piece back 56 ft from the crumbling cliff.

It is now a luxury B&B. The keeper's round room below the light can be rented for a unique experience.

Sussex Coast Road

48. *Aerial view of Belle Tout Lighthouse*

49. Seven Sisters and Birling Gap

Birling Gap

Half a mile further along we find Birling Gap. A steel staircase here is one of the few places that gives us access to the beach below the cliffs. For decades, Birling Gap has been very popular for a day out swimming, sunning on the beach or hiking along the cliff tops.

The family run Birling Gap Hotel entertained thousands of visitors every year with a great pub and restaurant. The cliffs eroding at 3 feet per year ended their existence some years ago. For decades the locals have been trying to persuade the National Trust to put up erosion defences but to no avail. They prefer to have nature take its course.

For those of that persuasion, there is a nudist beach a bit to the west. Take a look at the terrace houses near the cliff's edge as they may not be there for very long. Eight coastguard cottages were built in 1878. Three have already been demolished. The remaining 5 are still inhabited. There are no plans to save them from their fate. The National Trust, which owns the site, maintains the stairs and runs a cafe and visitor centre. There are still half a dozen private homes just to the west of the centre. They will soon be seafront properties.

East Dean and Friston

A mile inland from Birling Gap are the twin villages of East Dean and Friston. As most of the land in this area is owned by the National Trust, there has been very little development. The communities are almost quintessential South Downs villages of 100 years ago. They each have classic churches surrounded by large graveyards, village greens and homey cottages.

As we enter East Dean from the south, we take the first left turn past

50. Tiger Inn, East Dean Green

the church and come to the village green. Besides a couple of cafes, we find the Tiger Inn. For 400 years, this pub has been quenching the thirst of weary travellers.

In pleasant weather we can enjoy sitting outdoors in the green and watch village life.

Wednesday is a good day to come, for the weekly market where local produce and crafts are available.

Watch out for the Sherlock Holmes Blue Plaque.

He retired here over 100 years ago. Pretty good for a fictional character.

52. Friston Church

51. East Dean in Winter

Sussex Coast Road   51

53. Friston Forest

54. Cuckmere River at Exceat

Proceeding through East Dean, to the A259, we turn left to meander through Friston. After you pass the Virgin Mary Church, on the left we have one of the most pleasant views on our drive. On the right, we find the Friston Forest, replanted with beeches a 100 years ago, and on the left is green Downs farmland running to the cliffs and the sea.

Exceat

Two miles down the road we come to Exceat on the Cuckmere River and the visitor's centre for Seven Sisters Country Park. Exceat village has not existed for nearly 700 years. First settled by the Saxons as a fishing village protected by the river valley.

This was followed by King Alfred the Great who used it as an important naval base against his ongoing war with the Danes. Then after the Norman conquest, William the Conqueror gave it to his half-brother Robert, Earl Mortain.

In 1347, the plague arrived and killed most of the inhabitants.

Because of French raids, the few remaining villagers soon deserted the village.

The village was rediscovered about 100 years ago and a stone marker was erected to mark its location.

Do not be put off by the bad vibes from the ancient village. The visitors centre offers information and a small cafe. For the more adventurous type, there is a canoe and paddle-board rental nearby. The river is gentle but be prepared to get wet. The Cuckmere River loops down the valley to the beach at the sea.

This is where Braveheart landed in the movie. The walk is easy and very enjoyable with sheep grazing and WWII pillboxes and tank defences scattered around. One story has it that they strung lights up the valley to confuse the German night bombers into thinking it was the port at Newhaven.

Another walk for WWII history buffs is through the forest to the remains of RAF Friston. It was originally a farm field but was quickly converted to an emergency landing strip. Later Hurricanes and Spitfires were stationed there for the defence of London. The anti-aircraft batteries were credited with downing German V1 flying bombs saving many lives.

We follow the A259 across the single lane bridge over the Cuckmere and in half a mile we arrive in the built-up area as we come to the town of Seaford.

55. *Pebble Beach, Seaford*

Chapter Six
Seaford to Rottingdean

56. Seaford

Seaford is a coastal town with a long history. On Seaford Head, the chalk down and cliff beside the town, are the remains of an iron age hill fort and a Roman burial ground. A local writer compiled a book about the 19th Century peculiar-looking house built halfway up the slope by an independent woman from London.

The home attracted interesting owners and guests. In the 1930s it was used as a vacation spot for single young women, many of them widows from WWI. After WWII it was converted into the Splash Point Hotel. The 1960s saw the end of Seaford as a big tourist destination and that house was eventually demolished.

All the remains, for now, is the brick boundary wall that will soon fall into the sea as the cliff erodes. A challenging golf course now graces the slopes.

Seaford probably got its name from the Saxons referring to a ford crossing over the River Ouse which, at that time, flowed through the town. The river formed a natural harbour under Seaford Head. It was during the Middle Ages, that Seaford came into its own. Oddly, it was never mentioned in the Domesday Book. In 1298, it became a 'Cinque Port' which meant it supplied ships and mariners to the crown in exchange for benefits.

57. *Cliff House*

58. *Seaford Head 1906*

Sussex Coast Road 59

59. Seaford Head

The town prospered with fishing, boat building and trade with the continent for a while. By the end of the 14th Century, plague and French raids had put an end to the prosperity. By the 16th Century, the winter storms and the shifting shingle beach had blocked most of the river and a new exit was cut by storm and man at Newhaven, 4 miles to the west.

In the early 19th Century, a Martello tower was built near the sea to protect the coast from a French Napoleonic invasion. The restored tower is being put to good use as the town museum.

In the late 1800s, entrepreneurs decided to compete with Brighton and Eastbourne to make Seaford a seaside resort.

They built a better seawall and raised the roads. Some terraced houses and hotels were added but storms and flooding discouraged much further development. Because of the benefits of the sea air, convalescence homes and small private boarding schools became popular. WWI and WWII saw much military activity as a seaplane base, training centre and barracks. Canada's Calgary Tank Regiment was based here, protecting the coast

60. *Martello Tower Museum*

Sussex Coast Road 61

from German invasion and training for D-Day.

Now, this pleasant seaside community has become a dormitory town for Eastbourne, Brighton and even London.

A walk along the esplanade to the museum and Splash Point below Seaford Head is very enjoyable. The beach shingle rolling in the huge breakers on a stormy day can be heard throughout the town.

Tide Mills

Driving out of Seaford toward Newhaven, we turn left at Mill Drove on the seaward side. Driving down this road will get us to Tide Mills, an abandoned village that has a bit of history. Originally a mill was built here in the late 1700s to grind grain using the power of the tides.

It was upgraded in the next century and by 1850 over 50 men worked in the mill. They lived in the village with their families in company-built cottages.

The railway made shipping the flour to London via Newhaven a prosperous activity. The mill closed in 1883 and health and safety finally closed the village in 1939. The last residents were forcibly removed. In WWI it was used as a seaplane base to protect ships traveling to France from German U-Boats and in WWII for training in street fighting.

In the last 20 years, 2 novels have been written with Tide Mills as their locale. Some ruins of the village and mill still remain.

61. Remains of Tide Mills

62. Newhaven Lighthouse

Newhaven

The A259 swings inland a bit to avoid the harbour at Newhaven. Like Seaford, at the other end of Seaford Bay, there was a Bronze Age hill fort overlooking the town. When the storms of the 16th Century finally moved the shingle enough to close the harbour at Seaford the new channel was dug at the Saxon village of Meeching and became the new haven. A breakwater was built here to prevent the shingle from shifting again and closing up this harbour.

In the 1850s a fort was built for protection. With the arrival of the railway, cross channel ferries became active and have continued to this day. The town and port were very busy during WWI and WWII. The fort had ant- aircraft guns installed because of the frequent German bombing. As in Seaford, thousands of Canadian soldiers were stationed around here to protect the south coast. There is a memorial with a yearly commemoration ceremony for thousands of these soldiers who participated in the disastrous raid on the French port of Dieppe in August 1942

Historical characters include Louis Philippe I, the exiled king of France, who arrived in disguise in 1848 and murder suspect Lord Lucan, believed to have slipped onto a ferry in 1974. The fort and museum are worth visiting and if it is a warm sunny day a dip in the sea at Newhaven beach is a nice break.

63. *Looking at Newhaven beach from Fort Hill*

64. Newhaven Fort

Now back up to the A259 and we head for the next village.

Peacehaven

Peacehaven did not exist before WWI. In 1916, entrepreneur Charles Neville bought a large area of farmland above the cliffs 2 miles west of Newhaven and planned to develop the land and sell the individual lots. The original name for the town was New Anzac-on-Sea. After the disastrous campaign at Gallipoli where the Australians and New Zealanders suffered huge casualties, the name was quickly changed to Peacehaven.

The plots were inexpensive and originally had been planned for returning servicemen and their families. Because of the lower prices, nearly everyone could now afford a place by the sea. The first houses were built with any available materials that could be found including old railway coaches. With the installation of water and power in the 1920s, more permanent homes started to be built. The streets, which are all called avenues, are built on a grid system running straight down to the sea with only the A259 and another road bisecting them. There is no beach along these cliffs but there are stairs down and a lovely

Sussex Coast Road   65

Peacehaven Zero

walk by the sea.

There is also a clifftop walk along a paved promenade which will take us by another Peacehaven claim to fame. The town is on the zero meridian and has the monument to prove it. We have just passed from the east to the west (globally speaking).

Saltdean

Another couple of miles along gets us to the village of Saltdean. (Dean is Saxon for dip or valley.) The upmarket suburb village is mostly part of the city of Brighton and Hove although it is 5 miles away. From the shingle beach below the village, using the undercliff path we can walk all the way to the Palace Pier in Brighton.

Like Peacehaven, Saltdean was an invention of the entrepreneur Charles Neville who in the 1920s bought up some more farmland and developed them into lots. Unlike the grid in Peacehaven, the streets here were built around the central oval of Saltdean Park. It quickly became a seaside destination for the discerning vacationer in the interwar years.

The Saltdean Lido is a Grade II listed building constructed in 1937/38 in the Art Deco style of the

66. Saltdean Lido

times. It was built to help encourage the belief that sea air and exercise promoted health and energy. The Lido was and is now, considered the best lido in the UK. A couple of years after construction, WWII forced its closure as it was too dangerous with the Battle of Britain going on overhead. The bathers were once strafed by a German fighter. (He missed everyone.) The National Fire Service used it for training until the end of the war.

For years after, the lido was left to rot. Finally, in 1964 the city of Brighton refurbished and opened it. They also added a library and community centre. For the next 30 years, it was enjoyed by locals and tourists, bringing back some of the seaside resort atmosphere of the 30s. By the end of the 90s, it was becoming too expensive to maintain and a proposal in 2010, was to fill in the pools and build apartments. A local group (Save Saltdean Lido Campaign) raised awareness and funds and had it refurbished and reopened in all its original glory in 2017. Enjoy a swim and some history.

Built at the same time, the Grand Ocean Hotel quickly became the place to be seen by the royals, the rich and the famous. Opened in 1938, the now Grade II listed building was of the Streamline Moderne style. Having all the modern facilities, the guests would never have to leave to enjoy their holiday. As with the lido, WWII quickly forced it to close and it too was used by the firefighters as a training facility. Worse for wear, Billy Butlin bought it in 1953 and turned it into an upscale holiday

67. Grand Ocean Hotel

camp hotel. After 50 years of use, the hotel needed a major upgrade and in 2010, it was converted to luxury apartments. The building has gotten back some of its 30s Art Deco look.

Rottingdean

Rottingdean, unlike its eastern neighbours, has been a village for several thousand years. Turning right off the A259 up the High Street takes us through a traditional English village. The little shops are here beside old pubs and the duck pond in the village green. Like many of the old villages along this coast, it was very involved in smuggling, both ways, wines and spirits from France and Downs sheep wool back. Over the years it has been known for its exclusive finishing schools.

The village became popular with the 'arts' set who wanted to get out of London and could not tolerate the excesses of Brighton.

Near the centre of the village is a public park named for one of Rottingdean's most famous residents, Rudyard Kipling.

Kipling Gardens used to be the grounds for The Elms, the house he lived and wrote in. It was abandoned and overgrown until the local preservation society brought it back to life as a formal

English garden. A great place to stop and enjoy our lunch and the flowers at one of the benches.

Back to the A259 and we head for the Sussex coast's most famous city, Brighton. (Technically it is now called Brighton and Hove).

68. Rudyard Kipling's House

Chapter Seven
Brighton

Brighton

Known as 'Little London', Brighton has grown from a tiny Saxon farming and fishing village to a metropolis of over 300,000 people. It is possible it was the first and the most popular seaside resort in the UK, attracting millions of tourists every year.

Its story includes kings, aristocrats, the rich, celebrities, murderers and working-class families. It has seen its share of rock stars, youth gangs and mobsters. Riots and political bombings are not strangers here either. The city offers everything for the seaside resort, the beach, entertainment, hotels, old-fashioned B&Bs and the most popular pier in England.

One of the symbols and biggest attractions is the Royal Pavilion. It was built, in the Indian style, by King George IV (whilst still the Prince of Wales), for his longtime companion and lover, Maria Fitzherbert. It is fun to explore and learn its history. But we are just sticking to the coast road, called the Marine Parade.

The many interesting sights and places around Brighton could fill a book on its own. Starting from the east from Rottingdean, the first significant part of Brighton of note is the Brighton Marina. Brighton did not have a natural harbour, so boats had to moor offshore and smaller boats brought people and goods to the beach. In the 1800s the building of piers relieved this problem.

70. Brighton Marina

But, as the city grew, so did the demand for moorage. The marina was built in the 1970s and opened by Queen Elizabeth in 1979. Besides, moorage for 1,600 boats, the marina offers commercial and residential buildings. The marina offers the boating enthusiast a wonderful place to live, work and play.

The first street on our right as we head toward town is Boundary Road. From 1606 until 1928 this was the eastern boundary of Brighton. It was set to the large Black Rock that used to be found on the beach. At low tide, black rocks can still be found on the shore.

As with other seaside resorts, lidos or swimming pools were all the rage in the 1930s. At Black Rock, Brighton built its own in the popular Seaside Modern style of the time, complete with changing rooms, cafe and diving platform. Other than being closed during WWII, the heated seawater pool was very popular until they started to build the marina next door. The construction drove people away in the 1970s. It was demolished soon after when cracks were found in the pool.

On the land side opposite, we see what looks like a French chateau. The French Convalescent Home was opened in 1896 as a comfortable place for French nationals living in England. Paid for by France, they believed that the sea air would help the sick and aged live better away from the smog of London.

71. French Convalescent Home

During WWI it acted as a military hospital. In 1986 the local health authority took it over as a care home. In 1999 it was closed and sold. The new owners almost tore it down for a new apartment development. English Heritage quickly moved in and declared it a Grade II Listed Building. So the owners converted it into luxury apartments. It is still one of the few French-looking buildings in England. The nuns who ran it for 100 years finally got to go back to France.

After the chateau, we notice, on our right, the white four-storey houses of Lewes Crescent and Sussex Square. These magnificent Regency houses have been inhabited for nearly 200 years by famous notables. One of the most renowned was the author Lewis Carroll who lived at No. 11 from 1874 until 1887. As we drive along, we will find 2 more groups of Regency houses at Marine Square and Royal Crescent. Though not as big but still impressive, these homes have had their share of celebrities. Sir Lawrence Olivier had 2 houses joined together on Royal Crescent where he lived for many years.

On the beach side, we have the oldest running electric railway in the world. In its time it has been lengthened, shortened, almost destroyed by storms and still keeps on running. The mile ride along the beach from the marina to the pier is fun and offers an alternate view of the town.

Kemptown was developed in the early 1800s by Thomas Kemp as a residential estate just to the east of Brighton. Many of the Regency and Victorian houses have been converted into flats, clubs, bars and hotels. It is very popular with students and artists. A ten-minute walk gets us to the beach, the pier or the clubs downtown. Kemptown has been considered the gay capital of England for 200 years which adds to its flamboyant atmosphere. The largest pride parade in the country is held here every August. Come early, parking is atrocious.

One thing we cannot ignore is the history of the three Brighton Piers. The first, the Royal Suspension Chain Pier, was opened in 1823. Captain Samuel Brown who designed and built it was a suspension bridge expert. 'Chains' suspended between 4 towers held up the deck below. It was built as a landing stage for cargo boats and passengers. Fascination soon attracted visitors who wanted to stroll down the pier. This in turn attracted souvenir and candy kiosks and entertainment. Brown decided to charge an extravagant 2d entrance fee to keep the riff-raff out. By the 1830s, thousands of visitors came every day. By the 1840s, the railways severely cut into the shipping business but not to the tourists. The only limiting factor was the size of the pier deck. The West Pier build

73. *Kemptown Brewery*

Sussex Coast Road 75

74. Brighton Chain Pier c.1890s

in the 1860s was the final straw. The Chain Pier was closed in 1866 and in 1896 a great storm washed what was left out to sea. Almost a kind of revenge, the debris caused a lot of damage to the Palace Pier which was under construction at the time.

The second was the famous Brighton West Pier opened in 1866 purely as a tourist entertainment structure. It quickly became the main attraction to the seaside resort. Additions were built in 1894 and 1916. Just after WWI, it reached its visitor apex when it offered attractions and entertainment including live theatre, music, dances and restaurants. By this time it was getting competition from the Palace Pier, the third pier. It was noted that the locals preferred the West Pier and the Palace was the favourite of the day trippers. WWII saw the pier closed and some of the decking removed to thwart any German invasion. In 1944 an RAF fighter plane hit the pier. After the war, it never regained its popularity. Maintenance costs were crippling the 100-year-old pier's finances. In 1969 it became a Grade II listed building, but the owners could not afford the repair costs. It was finally completely closed in 1975. Several restoration attempts were made in the next 25 years but all failed. The storm in 1986 caused major structural damage and the access was cut in 1991. Two fires in 2003 put

75. The remains of Brighton West Pier, early morning

an end to any dreams of restoration. The pier has been collapsing piece by piece ever since. On a quiet, misty morning, the last of the remains can look like a ghost ship drifting just out to sea.

The third pier, opened in 1899, was originally named The Brighton Marine Palace and Pier. Today it is best known as the Palace Pier. It was immediately very popular with the tourists.

76. The remains of Brighton Palace Pier

Sussex Coast Road

77. Brighton Pavilion

In 1911 a musical pavilion was added and attracted performers like Laurel and Hardy and Charlie Chaplin. Except during the two World Wars, the pier has never lost its popularity. The post-WWII period saw change of owners several times and an updating of attractions. The top end of the pier has been changed into a funfair with rides including a merry-go-round and a rollercoaster. In 1971, it became a Grade II listed building.

The iconic structure has appeared in movies, books and TV shows. Still drawing millions of visitors every year, Palace Pier has become one of the best know symbols of Brighton and indeed England.

That gets us past the piers. Information about the Royal Pavilion, the Lanes and the many other features of Brighton is covered very well in so many articles, books and websites that we are going to skip most of those and relate a few stories about some of the lesser known or peculiar features.

If we leave the Royal Pavilion grounds by the north gate and cross the road, we get to the Victoria Gardens. At the north end is a lovely edifice that should be viewed after dark. The Mazda fountain has nothing to do with the car but was a brand of light bulb made by a British company at the beginning of the last century. The fountain was lovingly restored by a local lighting company

78. *Mazda Fountain*

in 2019 after being dark for 30 years. Using LED lights, the fountain's water jets have a rainbow of colours as they shoot up to 35 feet in the air. The company did it free of charge. The LED lights use less than 1% of the electricity of the old lights from the 1980s. Watching the light show can leave you mesmerized. Besides, it is only steps away from Ye Olde King and Queen, one of Brighton's most fascinating pubs, full of nooks and crannies, staircases, coats of arms and stained glass.

Moving along back on the waterfront, we come across another square of four-storey regency houses

Sussex Coast Road

with a bronze statue of a soldier blowing a bugle. This impressive plinth is dedicated to the Sussex soldiers who died in South Africa from 1900 to 1902. The park behind the bugler is a clever disguise for an underground parking lot. Good idea too as Brighton parking can be a nightmare.

Traveling further west we pass the Upside-Down House, the Beach Club and the Bandstand. When Brighton and Hove were two separate towns, the boundary was right here where we find the statue of the Angel of Peace. Catching it as the sun sets presents a wonderful sight. The angel holding up an olive branch is dedicated to King Edward VII who convalesced here a few times. He was known as the peacemaker. Unfortunately, the peace did not last long as two years after the statue was erected, WWI broke out across the channel.

That completes Brighton for this book. We did not touch on the riots, the Mods and Rockers, the gangsters and IRA bombings. The story of this tourist city by the sea has been the subject of many books.

Now on to the other half of Brighton, Hove.

79. Angel of Peace

80. Palmeira Square, Hove

Chapter Eight
Hove to Shoreham

Hove

Like many of the coastal towns, Hove was a small fishing village surrounded by open farmlands until the 19th Century. The only other industry was smuggling which came to a head in 1818 with a pitched battle on the beach between the smugglers and the revenue men. The town started to grow as Brighton spilled over its boundaries to accommodate the increased demand for seaside residences.

The residents on the Hove side indicated that their address was in Brighton and not the little decrepit town of Hove. The expansion quickly moved down the beach with the building of the usual elegant four-storey regency terrace houses around lovely parklike squares. As the town grew, the upper crust liked the wide boulevards and parks away from the hustle of Brighton. So when asked if you were from Brighton, you snobbishly replied, 'Yes, but Hove actually.'

81. Palmeira Square

82 Victorian ironwork covered seating

About a quarter of a mile from the Peace Angel, Palmeira Square stretches from the seaside up to Church Street. The houses around its sides are lovely examples of Victorian elegance. The park square's creation has a couple of stories. To level it, workers flattened a bronze age mound which turned out to be an ancient chief's grave. Along with an axe and dagger, an amber gobbet was found in the tree trunk coffin. This 3,000-year-old artifact indicates that there was trade at the time with Europe as the cup's origins are from the Baltic.

The square had another oddity in more recent times, only about 200 years ago. The Victorians had an obsession to build bigger structures usually with the new uses of iron. The Chain Pier in Brighton is a good example. In 1832 an English botanist and gardener started to build an iron and glass conservatory in Palmeira Square. He had failed to raise funds for one in Brighton so decided to build a bigger one in Hove covering 1 1/2 acres. Unfortunately, the engineering was not up to the task and the day before the official opening in 1833, when the supporting scaffolding was removed, the iron could not support the weight and it came crashing down. Luckily, no one was hurt except for the botanist who is said to have gone blind from shock. The builders quickly left the country. The ruins supplied Hove with a tourist attraction for the next 20 years until they were finally removed.

Another quarter of a mile along

84. Hove Beach Huts

the coast, we find something old and something new. The channel side of Hove is lovely because it has been left as lawns. The paved promenade between the lawns and the beach is a great place for walking or jogging and it has been for many decades. Along the edge of the walkway, we find the multi-coloured beach huts. The Victorians loved to walk along here too and often stopped to enjoy the view.

The city built decorative beach shelters with benches and glass so the visitors could enjoy the view and sea air away from the harsh elements. It is said they were enjoyed even by the royalty. Some of these shelters have been renovated and still decorate the seafront. We can find one near a new artwork called the Hove Plinth. The sculpture atop has the look of a planetary model except the planets are local symbols. The sculpture is supposed to be replaced every 18 months.

There are many other fascinating things to see in Hove. On a rainy day, a stop in at the extensive Hove Museum and Art Gallery keeps us dry and entertained.

Following the A259 (Kingsway) another half mile past the artificial lagoon and we come to Portslade-on-Sea which is a suburb of Hove. On the channel side, we notice the top end of Shoreham Harbour.

Shoreham-by-Sea

This stretch of the road from Portslade to the ancient town of New Shoreham has some interesting features. We can hardly miss the chimney of the power plant on the far side of the port which is a beacon for many miles around. Portslade is very industrial with many warehouses and small manufacturing companies lining both sides of the harbour, not pretty but good for the local economy. The port is the largest between Dover and Plymouth and has been used for hundreds of years. Vessel size restrictions limit its capacity and larger ships cannot be handled.

As we get to where the River Adur enters the channel, we have an interesting configuration. The river is flowing from west to east parallel to the coast from where the shifting sands and pebbles have formed a spit of land over many years. On the east side is the entrance to the port but still considered to be part of the river. There are tidal locks here in order to maintain the water level in the inner harbour. This restricts access to six-hour periods twice a day as the tides change.

Another mile down the A259 gets us past the big box stores and the marina and into the old town. Although Shoreham is much smaller than its neighbours, there was a time

85 Old Shoreham

86. *Shoreham lifeboat station and lighthouse*

87. *St Mary de Haura Church*

Sussex Coast Road

during the Middle Ages when it was much larger and far more important than the local villages. Because of this, it has a huge Norman church, St Mary de Haura. The church was built by one of William the Conqueror's friends for a monastery in France. This Grade I listed building still serves as the parish church and is a real surprise to see such an impressive building in a small town.

The best way to see the next part of this town is on foot. Walking back to the A259 from the church along the pedestrianized East Street we come to the new Adur Ferry Bridge which in 2013 replaced the old Adur Ferry Bridge which probably replaced the Adur ferry. The walk across the pedestrian bridge on a sunny day is lovely and we get a good look at the river with its boats and marinas. The old town is behind us and Shoreham Beach in front. There is more to see in town, so we walked back and turned left to find our next attraction in a few hundred feet.

A 'must see' is the Marlipins Museum right on the corner of Middle Street and the A259, not far from the church. The chessboard pattern building made of flint and Caen stone is hard to miss. Having been built near the end of the 12th Century makes it one of the oldest non-religious buildings in England.

88. *Marlipins Museum*

89 New Ferry Bridge

Sussex Coast Road   89

What it was built for is up for debate. We have been told it could have been a warehouse, a courthouse, a market or a chapel. Better suggestions include part of a priory or a meeting place for the Knights Templar. Thankfully in 1922 it was purchased by the Sussex Archaeological Society and converted to a museum. The 2,500 items on display show everything from pre-Roman times to the shipbuilding of the last century. A tour of the museum, inside, outside and structurally is well worth our time.

Back to the car and we drive west out of town. Cross the bridge and at the first roundabout we took the first exit and headed toward the sea. The road quickly turns left and we are headed back toward Shoreham but on the other side of the river on the spit that is Shoreham Beach. Before WWI, Britain's fledgling silent movie industry used Shoreham Beach for many of their movies because of the excellent light.

After the first war, with housing being at a premium, people moved to the beach and built bungalows out of

90. *Shoreham Redoubt*

anything they could find, including old train carriages and scraps of wood. Bungalow Town grew even though there was no electricity or water.

The west end of the spit attracted many theatre and film people between jobs. With the fear of invasion during WWII, this shanty town was evacuated with larger houses torn down and smaller ones boarded up. After the war, a well laid out town was developed and all that remains are old pictures and memories of a unique way of life.

At the end of the spit, overlooking the River Adur's mouth, is the Shoreham Redoubt. The fort was completed in 1857 to protect the harbour from attack from France. It was built with a wall and ditch facing the sea. Within 10 years the big guns were declared obsolete and the fort ineffective as it was vulnerable to attack from land. The guns were upgraded but the fort remained the same. This is where the 'light' was right for the pre-WWI movie makers and used to film at least 4 silent films. During WWII it was used as part of a shore battery. For many years after the war, it fell into disuse until the county council tried some restoration in the late 70s. For the last ten years, the volunteer group Friends of Shoreham Fort has been restoring the redoubt and hope to make it a local attraction.

Back the way we came and on to the next town, Lancing.

91. Lancing College Chapel

92. Looking towards Lancing College Chapel from Shoreham Footbridge

Chapter Nine
Lancing to Goring-by-Sea

Richard Powell

Lancing

Lancing was another of the 18th Century seaside resort favoured by the gentry who wanted a place that offered peace and quiet. The shingle beach stretches for miles and offers a beautiful spot to spend the summer. The farmlands around the village were very popular for supplying market crops for Brighton market and London's Covent Garden. With easy and frequent access, it became a dormitory community for many who worked in London. There is little of the old village left. Remains of an ancient temple on the Roman Road above the village offer us views over the town, the Downs and the channel.

If we look up above Lancing, we see the distinctive chapel of Lancing College. It has been a public school since 1848 and currently teaches 600 boarding and independent day students. It sits on a hill above the Shoreham airport in the South Downs overlooking the Adur River. There is a holy well within the grounds that predates Christianity. The chapel soaring over 100 feet high is visible for miles along the coast. Built of Sussex sandstone it contains a beautifully vaulted ceiling, stained glass and the tomb of its founder. Very impressive and open to the public at times.

Along the beach, past Brooklands Park and Lake, we come to Worthing which has absorbed most of Lancing.

93. *Worthing Marine Gardens and Winchelsea Garden on the seafront*

Worthing

The area around Worthing has seen human activity since the Bronze Age. There are traces of a flint mine nearby and when we look up to the highest hills on the Downs above the city, we see the remains of hill forts used until Roman times. The original settlement was a tiny village of fewer than 100 people. It took until the 18th Century to reach 2,000 inhabitants and that was due to the new fad for healthy sea air. In the middle part of that century, developers started building seafront homes for the wealthy of the time. What really kicked it off was when in 1798, King George III's daughter, Princess Amelia, spent time sea bathing in Worthing, while recuperating from consumption (tuberculosis). The king would not let his daughter stay in Brighton, as it was considered too racy. Gentility built their seaside homes in the quickly expanding community. Second only to Brighton for size, the current population exceeds 110,000 people. There is constant competition with its larger companion just down the coast.

As we approach central Worthing, the A259 veers slightly inland away from the coast. Just ahead on our left, we cannot miss the historic Grade II listed 'Beach House' villa. Build around 1820, it has been owned and lived in by the head of the London police force (Bow Street Runners), an MP, a playwright and

94. *Beach House Villa*

other various lords and ladies. King Edward VII stayed there at least 10 times on his visits to Worthing. In 1937, it became home to 60 Spanish children evacuated during Spain's civil war and later by the Air Corps during WWII. The grounds down to the beach were purchased by Worthing Council in 1927 for public use.

Just across the road is the Beach House Park. These 10 acres of land were bought by the council and converted to a public park in the 1920s. The back part is used as bowling greens, but the interesting part is in the front. A beautiful formal garden is maintained with a memorial in the centre. This unique memorial is not for soldiers but 'Warrior Birds'. It was dedicated in 1950 to the pigeons that died in WWII in service to the military. Different.

Another quarter of a mile gets us to the town centre. The road here comes to a T junction with pedestrianised shopping in front of us. Turning right follows the A259, but we want to stick by the coast, so we turn left and follow the gardens down to Marine Parade where we turn right toward the pier. Before we do that, we want to stop and take in Steyne Gardens, which is the town-centre park.

It is a lovely open green space running down to the sea with three or four-storey classic apartment buildings and hotels around it.

Memorial for Warrior Birds

96. *Worthing Pier*

97. *Worthing Pier c.1900*

96 Richard Powell

This open square is used frequently for festivals and fayres. From November to the end of February the city erects a covered ice rink at the north end of the gardens.

A short distance along the seafront we come upon Worthing's award-winning pier. In 2019, it won the Pier of the Year award for the second time because it was so well maintained by the Worthing Council. This Grade II, Art Deco structure as with most piers along the coast has had its share of ups and downs. Originally opened in 1862 it became very popular with tourists. To celebrate Queen Victoria's jubilee, the pier was cleaned up and a pavilion was added to the end. Over the years, this building was used as ballroom, theatre, restaurant and nightclub. The middle section was destroyed by the Easter storm of 1913 but was quickly rebuilt. It too, like most of the channel coast piers during WWII suffered the indignation of having the deck in the middle torn up to prevent being used in a German invasion. Today it still attracts thousands of tourists and locals for a peaceful stroll on a summer's day.

Just at the entrance to the pier is one of the three theatres run by the local council. The Pavilion Theatre is a lovely domed structure, opened in 1926. It contains a cafe and bar and hosts entertainment with everything from pantomimes to burlesque to musicals and circuses.

The other two theatres, the Connaught and the Dome also provide entertainment with beautifully styled and decorated buildings.

98. *Pavilion Theatre*

The cultural scene in Worthing has been and still is very active. There are many reasons people prefer Worthing over Brighton, not least that it isn't Brighton. The larger city offers excitement and activity while the 'Little Sister' is quieter and offers a more relaxed and affordable lifestyle. There is always a nice quiet spot-on Worthing's Beach. Shopping is easier as is parking. The Royal Arcade, opened in 1925, offers over 20 shops under cover in an Edwardian style. The cost of living is lower and there is less crime.

Following the Marine Parade for a mile, we pass the expected and now familiar white Regency and Victorian seaside houses favoured by the wealthy of the times. Many have been converted to apartments, small hotels and restaurants with pleasant views of the beach and channel. Another half mile along this drive gets us past some new apartments and houses.

At the bottom of Grand Avenue on the beach side is a memorial to the soldiers stationed here during WWII.

Next on the right, we see the very popular Marine Gardens, a lovely place to stop and enjoy the formal gardens and a cup of coffee.

Following along a bit, to a roundabout, we take the first exit, which leads us north. Turning left again, at the first road, we are on Marine Crescent, except now we are in Goring-by-Sea.

100. Worthing Seafront

Goring-by-Sea

Goring became Goring-by-Sea in 1908 so as not to be confused with Goring-on-Thames. Streets and houses are laid out quite symmetrically from the semicircular park in the centre above the shingle beach. This quiet town is a suburb of Worthing, but it is not without its interesting points. We are going to have to leave the sea for now and head inland to rejoin the A259. When we come to the roundabout at Sea Lane we turn right and follow this street with trees down the middle boulevard for about a mile. At the next roundabout, we again turn right. The huge oak trees on our left and around the church are Mediterranean Holm Oaks, planted here in the 19th Century. The A259 is directly in front of us and we turn left and continue for another half mile. On our left is the English Martyrs Catholic Church which has a fascinating feature. If we want to see the ceiling painted in the Sistine Chapel in Vatican City we can do it here.

The ceiling of this church has a 2/3 scale reproduction of the one in Italy. A sign painter parishioner spent five and a half years painting this marvel.

We continue along to the next roundabout and again turn right. In half a mile, we come to a large roundabout and turn left this time. We have now left Goring and are heading for our next stop.

101. Sistine Ceiling at Goring

102. Ferring Seafront

Chapter Ten
Ferring to Littlehampton

Ferring, Kingston, Preston, Rustington

Along the route, there is a series of villages between Worthing and Littlehampton. These ancient villages go back to Saxon times where they supported farming and fishing for centuries. There we find some lovely old Norman churches and manor houses. Only in the last 100 years have they attracted more people looking for a quiet place by the sea as a commuter village, a vacation spot or retirement community. There are green gaps used for farming on both sides of Ferring. Construction here has been limited and helps give the town more of a village feel.

103. Goring Gap, aerial view looking north of the West Sussex farming area between Goring and Ferring

104. Rustington Convalescent home c1900

Littlehampton

We drive along the A259 for about 5 km, passing some big box stores and farmland and come to a big roundabout. Over on our right is the world headquarters for the Body Shop. We are not going there. We take the second exit onto Horsham Road with a large cemetery on our left, now heading for the sea at Littlehampton. Following this road for about a half mile. it starts to curve to the right. We do not go that way but keep going straight ahead toward the sea. Careful as we have to turn left across traffic. On down St. Floras Road for ¼ mile to a roundabout where we take the first exit, a hundred feet to a small roundabout where we take the second exit onto Norfolk Road and straight down to the channel. The sea at last where we find a convenient parking lot. It is time to walk a bit.

Littlehampton got its name so as not to be confused with the larger town of Southampton further down the coast. Like most of the villages along the coast, it started as a farming and fishing village before Roman, then Saxon and then Norman times. The Arun River, which flows into the sea here, was navigable up

Sussex Coast Road

to the castle at Arundel but silted up often so a harbour was built at Littlehampton. The 17th and 18th centuries changed the community from a small village into a prosperous seaside town. It attracted its share of the rich and aristocracy and even had a channel ferry to France. The popularity continued into the 20th Century when it was nicknamed 'The Children's Paradise'. Even today in the summer, busloads of day-trippers come down from London for a day at the sea.

The town has some interesting sites to explore. From the parking lot turn left along the beachside walkway. On the right, the beach stretches out for miles in either direction but what is lovely are the hundreds of brightly painted beach huts. Walk on toward the village of Rustington and we discover the 19th Century convalescence home. Used for 150 years, this impressive building was a place to recover from surgery and illnesses.

Patients in 'bath' chairs were wheeled out onto the lawns and conservatoires to get the sun and breathe the healthy sea air. Even today, it is used by people recovering from illness or operations.

Back the way we came and near the parking lot, we discover a strange looking building which is almost impossible to describe. The East Beach Cafe is made of iron welded into its odd shape and has done a wonderful job of rusting.

105. Beach Huts

106. East Beach Café

Further along the promenade is Britain's longest bench. For 324 metres, the slats twist and loop in a weird pattern. The idea was based on a design from local school children and made possible by a government grant.

Looking back toward the town we find the East Beach Green which hosts all sorts of activities throughout the year including bonfire night, summer outdoor movies, picnics, fayres and festivals. Following the beach walk to the Arun River, we find the Lifeguard station and the much-photographed little lighthouse on the short pier that guards the entrance to the river. On our right, along the river is a funfair.

For 90 years is has been a big draw for the children, no matter what age. Originally opened in 1932 by Billy Butlin, it was popular for the Wild Mouse roller coaster situated on the top of the building. Sold in 1977, it has undergone major renovations.

Behind the funfair is a circular artificial lake in a lovely park.

107. Longest Bench

Sussex Coast Road

108. *Littlehampton Harbour*

109. *Coloured Houses Littlehampton*

110. *Littlehampton Beach*

111. Oyster Pond c.1910

Built in 1910 to hold oysters, the Oyster Pond immediately attracted people to sit and enjoy the view or watch as kids sailed model boats or used nets to catch little crabs. The oysters are gone but the lake and park, complete with benches and sculptures still attract tourists and locals. A short walk, up Pier Road, are what has been rated as a couple of the best fish and chips shops in England. We can enjoy our meal watching the boats on the river or back at the Oyster Pond surrounded by the ever-present seagulls. The harbour has many other sights to enjoy. Littlehampton is a good place for a family day out.

Time to see the other side of the river, so we head back to the car. Leaving Littlehampton, we cross the River Arun. At the second road on the left, Ferry Road, we turn left and head back toward the sea. There are a couple more things to investigate. Almost back to the river, taking the first turn on the right, Rope Walk. We follow the road past the golf course and the yacht club until we come to the end at West Beach. Before us is a soft sandy beach with very few people to disturb us. We also find something we have not seen since Camber Sands, dunes. The area is protected because of its rare plants, animals, birds and reptiles.

112. Littlehampton Harbour

115. West Beach Littlehampton

We stick to the boardwalk so as not to disturb their natural habitat.

Just behind the beach and half buried in the sand is Littlehampton Fort. Similar to the one near Shoreham, this fort was built in 1854 to protect the River Arun from attack from France. It never saw any use in the 19th Century and was soon obsolete. The last time it was used was during WWII. In the last 10 years, extensive work has been done by a very active group of volunteers to get the crumbling, overgrown fort restored to its former self. It is interesting to see the design and technology of the mid-19th Century.

That is it for Littlehampton, as we retrace our path back. Turning left, we head for Bognor Regis.

114. Littlehampton Fort

Sussex Coast Road

115. Aerial view of Littlehampton

116. Felpham seafront

Chapter Eleven
Felpham to Pagham

About three miles along from Littlehampton, just past Worm's Wood, at the roundabout, we take the first exit onto Flansham Road (B2259). The A259 runs on toward Chichester but we are headed for Felpham.

Felpham

At the next roundabout turn to the right still following the B2259. In about half a mile we turn left down Felpham Road and pass the church and the old part of the village. For those of us interested in cultural history, we can turn left at Vicarage Lane and come to William Blake's Home. He lived here from 1800 to 1803 where he wrote the epic poem, Milton. The house is open to the public and the local society has many events here.

Felpham is another of the ancient villages along the coast that go back to pre-Saxon times, supporting a bit of farming, fishing and later smuggling. It is older than Bognor but now serves as a suburb of the larger town. Prior to 1066, the village was valued at £ 10. During medieval times much of the coast was eroded and fields and pastures were lost. Shore defences and goynes helped slow the loss of land. Felpham has a typical Sussex beach with pebbles at high tide and sand when low. The village was slow to attract seaside resort development but in the last 100 years, most of the land from the old village to the beach

117 William Blake's Cottage

118. Felpham seafront

has been filled with houses occupied by retirees and those looking for a quiet, less expensive place than Bognor.

Speaking of which let us follow Felpham Road, as it turns into Upper Bognor Road, and we see our first object of note in Bognor.

Bognor Regis

We have come this way because we wanted to see just how big the Bognor Butlin's Holiday camp is. Opened in 1960 by Billy Butlin, it has grown to 60 acres with three large hotels being added in the last 15 years. The seaside camp, open all year, attracts over 385,000 guests annually.

Only three of all the Butlin's camps are left. This is the largest seaside resort in the south of England. Most of the others were closed in the 1980s and 90s because of overseas competition.

Love them or hate them, this is a part of 20th Century British vacation culture. The story of Billy Butlin, a WWI Canadian veteran soldier, who created British family camp vacations in the 1920s is a great story and worth researching.

119. Butlin's Bognor

Like many of the other coastal towns, Bognor was built as a seaside resort in the late 18th Century by Richard Hotham. He wanted to call it Hothamton but it did not catch on. The town did not grow much until the railway arrived in the 1860s. Hotham is remembered by a very lovely park bearing his name, right beside Butlins. The road continues down to the Esplanade with the Victorian residences on the right and the beach and sea on the left.

In 1929 King George V went to Bognor to speed his recovery from lung surgery. It sounds like he was not too impressed with the town because when he was petitioned to add the suffix 'Regis' to the town's name, his reply was 'Bugger Bognor'. They were granted the request, so the official name is Bognor Regis.

Like most of the major towns along the coast a pier was built at Bognor and opened in 1865 where it stretched 1,000 feet into the channel. Over the next 60 years, improvements were added including a pavilion, a large music hall at the seaward end and Bognor's first movie theatre. Charlie Chaplin and Gracie Fields entertained the crowds in their heydays. Storms did their damage here with the worst one in 1964 that destroyed the pavilion at the seaward end. About 600 feet of the weakened pier collapsed into the sea in 1999. Now the Grade II listed structure operates as a nightclub and bar. The Edwardian theatre is still quite a sight to see.

The pier had slightly different life to the other coastal piers during WWII. As with most of the south coast piers, parts were removed in the middle to discourage German's using it for an invasion. This pier was unique in that it was the only one the navy took over and it was called HMS Barbara. It was used as a training site for anti-aircraft guns and cannons. The theatres were used as lecture halls. The pavilion at the end where the gunnery training took place was accessed by a rope bridge. Unfortunately, low quality steel was used after the war to reconstruct the pier which added to its latter collapse in subsequent storms.

Just to the west of the pier, is The Steyne. This street has a garden running down the middle and is as peaceful now as it was when it was laid out in the 1820s. The three-storey buildings arranged neatly on both sides of the gardens offered some of the best accommodations of the time for the seaside visitors. In 1824 the 'Bath House' was opened in the street and offered the only place in town where you could get a cheap, hot bath.

120. Bognor Pier

121. Bognor Regis

In the 1890s, a local chemist noticed that there was no drinking fountain for the large number of children in the area. As the council was more interested in Queen Victoria's 60th anniversary than the needs of children, he publicly raised £111 and had the fountain built at the bottom end of the Steyne, near the promenade. For an unknown reason it was moved, in 1928, to Waterloo Square, opposite the pier.

In 1956, it was dismantled again and moved to Hotham Park, where it sat, dismantled for 10 years. In 1967, a local developer again raised public funds to have it reassembled. So now, we will find the Queen Victoria Jubilee children's fountain in a place near where it started, at the sea end of The Steyne.

Bognor and its neighbour Pagham had an interesting part in the D-Day operations during WWII.

122. Drinking Fountain

Learning from the mistakes of the Dieppe raid in 1942, the military realized that taking a port town in France would be almost impossible. So they decided to build a portable harbour and float it over to France following the landing. Sections of these floating docks were built near here and when they were put in the water just offshore, they were sunk so the Germans could not see them.

As D-Day approached they were refloated and towed to France after the invasion. One of the pontoon pieces known as a Beetle can be seen along West Beach at Bognor and a larger Mulberry part is in 100 feet of water off Pagham. It has become a diving attraction.

Now we have to double back toward Chichester. We follow the B2166 and B2259 until we meet up with the A259 at a roundabout. A few miles further, at the next roundabout the road joins the A27. We are now at the city of Chichester, which is a wonderful place to visit but is not really a coastal city.

125. *Mulberry Harbour Wreckage*

Sussex Coast Road   119

124 Aerial panorama of Chichester City Centre

Chapter Twelve
Chichester to Thorney Island

Chichester

In 43AD the Roman Emperor Claudius sent an army to conquer England they landed at Noviomagus which is present day Chichester. Within a few years, they had subdued most of England. They also constructed roads, one from here to Londinium so that supplies and troops could easily be moved from the south coast. After the Romans left the town fell into ruin but was eventually rebuilt by the Saxons and later by the Normans.

Chichester still has parts of the original Roman walls, a great Norman cathedral and many other historical buildings. Great place to spend a day exploring.

Following the A27 to the second roundabout which is posted as the A286, (Stockbridge Road), we leave at the first exit and head toward the sea.

125. A closer look at Chichester Cathedral

Sussex Coast Road 121

Chichester Harbour

Chichester Harbour has had human habitation for over 6,000 years. The Romans used it as the landing point when they conquered England. Saxons and then Normans have used the ports for trade and smuggling for centuries. With the advent of rail transport, the ports use faded and the harbour silted up.

In 1964, Chichester Harbour was designated an Area of Outstanding Natural Beauty (AONB). Most of the harbour is now a nature reserve which has prevented a lot of development and now the marshlands are home to tens of thousands of birds. Sailing, cycling, rambling and swimming make this a very popular stop for visitors.

126. Sailboats and Saltmarsh

127. Dell Quay

Dell Quay

Chartered as a 'port', Dell Quay handled much of the shipping for Chichester which was two miles away.

Today all that remains is a dozen houses, a 16th Century pub and the marina with the boat club. It is a lovely spot to stop for a meal and to enjoy the views of the harbour and the passing boats.

128. Walkway at East Head

East and West Wittering

Following the A286 takes us to the two villages of East and West Wittering. Inhabited since Saxon times, they are hugely popular with visitors because of the unobstructed miles of sandy, shallow beach which is perfect for surfing. Having turned the corner at Selsey Bill, we are now looking at the waters of the Solent and not the Channel. As we follow the beach, as it turns toward Chichester Harbour, we come to an area called 'The Hinge at East Head Spit'. England has such great place names.

Just around the corner, we come to the National Trust owned 'East Head'. This small nature reserve is home to sand dunes, rare lizards and salt marshes. If we tire of the secluded sandy beaches, there is the boardwalk through the middle of this enchanted landscape.

The area attracts more than surfers and day trippers. A number of celebrities including Kate Winslet, Keith Richards and Michael Ball have homes here. A great place for those who wish to find some peace and seclusion away from the cities.

Itchenor

Working our way back up toward Chichester we find Itchenor, which is a pretty village on the eastern shores of the Chichester Harbour. Believed to have been established by the Romans, it was active during Saxon and Norman times. Almost wiped out by the black death, it managed to survive and become a shipping port. Because of its beauty and location, the London 'well to do', who liked to sail, started building summer homes here in the late 19th Century. Today over 40% of the houses are classified as second homes.

This has changed the character of the village.

In the 70's, the village store, post office and primary school closed due to the dwindling permanent population. In 2020 the average house price was in excess of £1.3m making it the most expensive village in England.

The conservancy for the Chichester Harbour Reserve is run from Itchenor. They are responsible for managing the coexistence of wildlife and human recreation. For the rambler who wants a different perspective of the harbour, the conservancy maintains a dozen walking trails of various lengths.

The Itchenor Ferry has been running for over 400 years. (not the same boat).

cc-by-sa/2.0 - The Street, West Itchenor by Rob Farrow - geograph.org.uk/p/3545351

129 Itchenor Village

It currently runs in the summer on demand from the village to Bosham a mile further up the inlet. This ferry ride is part of one of the walks. There are longer harbour tours available for those who do not have access to a boat.

We now return to the A27 and at the next exit follow the A259 once again.

Fishbourne

Like Dell Quay, Fishbourne was a busy port for Chichester but as the estuary silted up and the railway proved a cheaper means of transport, Fishbourne village lost its importance. As early as 1805 locals had been finding pieces of Roman ruins but in the 1960s excavations of the largest Roman Palace in England brought back fame to Fishbourne.

The Roman house covers an area larger than Buckingham Palace. Every time they excavated some of the ruins, they found even more. Building of the palace started soon after the Roman occupation in the 1st Century. It was extended over several hundred years and finally abandoned around 270 AD after a major fire. Some of the palace will never be recovered as it is under the A27 and some of the nearby houses. The property has been opened to the public and not only shows the beauty of the floor mosaics but contains a museum with models that describe the workings of this huge complex.

In excavating the Roman ruins, archaeologists discovered thousands of artifacts that predate the Romans to the Iron Age and earlier. Flint tools found here could be over 6,000 years' old.

130. Fishbourne Palace Model

131. Fishbourne Palace Mosaic

Bosham

Off again on the A259 for another mile and at the roundabout, we take the first left onto Delling Lane and head for Bosham.

Bosham's recorded history starts with the Romans who used it as a major port and built homes and other buildings there.

Around 1800 part of the largest Roman statue built in England was found near here. It is believed that it is the head of Emperor Trajan, erected by Hadrian at the mouth of the harbour. After years in the Bishop of Chichester's garden, it was moved to the city's museum where it is now on display.

Saxon times saw much activity with a small monastery recorded here in the 7th Century and the church being built in the 9th Century, probably on top of a Roman structure.

This was replaced a couple of hundred years later with a larger one.

132. Bosham Harbour

This thousand-year-old Saxon church is still in use today.

There is a legend that a Danish raiding party stole the tenor bell from the church bell tower. As they were leaving, the other bells in the church started to chime and the tenor bell answered, destroying the Danish ship. On some quiet days when the church bells ring, the bell in the harbour still answers.

Another legend has King Canute and his drowned daughter buried under the floor of the church. There is also a story that King Harold was buried here after dying at the battle of Hastings. At the time of the writing of the Domesday Book, Bosham was described as one of the wealthiest villages in England.

Bosham was made notable again by the Sky Documentary series, Killer in My Village. An unsolved murder happened in the village in 2013 when Valerie Graves, a 55-year-old artist, was found bludgeoned to death. She was house sitting at a friend's home in Smugglers Lane and was found by her sister Janet on December 30. It was not until 2019 that someone was finally convicted of her murder.

133. Bosham

The investigation was sad but interesting and we had to research to find out whodunnit.

It is a very pretty village today attracting artists, photographers. cyclists, sailors and walkers. We got a sense of history exploring the village and browsing its craft shops.

There are a few more smaller villages and the military base at Thorney Island that make up the west side of the harbour. Most of these are part of the nature reserve and some places can only be accessed by footpaths.

So ends the A259 in Sussex.

134. Bosham

End of the Road

That is our trip along the Channel coast on the A259 from Rye to Chichester Harbour. For those who live here, I hope I have encouraged you to explore your county and look at it in a new light. Some of us have visited this strip of land and sea many times over the years and have enjoyed its sites and delights.

Hopefully, for those who have never been here, I have given you some insight into what to expect if you do visit. From the high green South Downs to endless miles of pebble beaches to busy seaside resorts, this area has so much to offer that we will keep coming back and finding something new or maybe very old. Enjoy the ride.

135. Seven Sisters

List Of Figures & Acknowledgements

1. **Detail from a Postcard Map of Sussex 3** © Alwyn Ladell, 2012, on Flickr - Alwyn Ladell has given reprint permission for scanned postcard. Original card printed by J. Salmon Ltd. in 1983. Company no longer exists.
2. **Camber Sands Beach 4** © JJ Jones - Panaramio – Wikimedia - Creative Commons Attribution 3.0 Unported license, reviewed on 21 January 2017
3. **A view of boats moored on the River Rother in the town of Rye, Sussex 5** © Nicola, Adobe Stock
4. **Rye and Camber Tramway - 'Victoria' with train crosses Broadwater Bridge (1914) 6** © Ken Clark's Archive, Wikimedia
5. **Camber Sands 7** © Adobe Stock, Andy
6. **Mermaid Street, Rye 8** © BazViv - Panaramio – Wikimedia - Creative Commons Attribution 3.0 Unported license, reviewed on 4 December 2016
7. **Mermaid Inn 9** © Nigel Wiggins, Adobe Stock
8. **Ypres Tower Museum 10** © 2015 Leonard Bentley. Wikimedia - Creative Commons Attribution-Share Alike 4.0 International license.
9. **Camber Castle 11** © 2014 Barbara van Cleve. Wikimedia - Creative Commons Attribution-Share Alike 4.0 International license.
10. **Rye Marshes 12** © David EP Dennis, Adobe Stock
11. **St Thomas the Martyr church and village cross, Winchelsea 13** © Julian Gazzard, Adobe Stock
12. **Winchelsea, St Thomas, Window 14** © IC (via Rick Powell)
13. **Walk over Pett Level with Hog Hill in the background 15** © SuxxesPhoto, Adobe Stock
14. **St. Thomas the Martyr 16** © 2019 Immanuel Giel. Wikimedia - Creative Commons CC0 1.0 Universal Public Domain Dedication
15. **Fishing Boats on East Beach 17** © 2015 Kevin Tuck, rgbstock
16. **Stade Beach Fisherman's Dinghy 18** © IC (via Rick Powell)
17. **Fishermen's Huts 18** © 2015 Kevin Tuck, rgbstock
18. **East Hill funicular railway station 19** © 2022 John Goodwin
19. **East Hill Well 19** © 2022 John Goodwin
20. **East Hill funicular railway station 20** © 2022 John Goodwin
21. **The view from the East Hill funicular railway 21** © 2022 John Goodwin
22. **Hastings Castle 22** © Ariadna de Raadt, Adobe Stock
23. **Hastings Castle 23** © Scott Bufkin, Adobe Stock
24. **Hastings Beach front with Hastings Castle on the hill, behind 23** © pxl.store, Adobe Stock
25. **Hastings Seafront 1934 24** © 2013 Phil Sellens. Wikimedia - Creative Commons Attribution 2.0 Generic license
26. **Hastings Pier 1966 Embroidery Exhibition 25** © Chris Roberts Wikimedia - CC Att-Share Alike 4.0 Int license
27. **Hastings Old Pier 26** © 2014 Phil Sellens Wikimedia - Creative Commons Attribution 2.0 Generic license
28. **St Leonards on Sea Beach Front 27** © cheekylorns, Adobe Stock
29. **St. Leonards-on-Sea Pier 28** © 2014 Phil Sellenss. Wikimedia - Creative Commons Attribution 2.0 Generic license
30. **Marine Court 29** © 2005 Nick Lott. Wikimedia - Creative Commons Attribution 2.0 Generic license
31. **Battlefield and Abbey 30** © Doro Hof/Wirestock, Adobe Stock
32. **Bexhill, Glyne Gap 31** © 2018 Dr-Mx. Wikimedia - Creative Commons CC0 1.0 Universal Public Domain Dedication
33. **De La Warr Pavilion 32** © 2006 Oliver Tookey. Wikimedia - Creative Commons Attribution-Share Alike 4.0 International license
34. **Bexhill Seafront Mansions 33** © 2015 Ben Bender. Wikimedia - Creative Commons Attribution-Share Alike 3.0 Unported license
35. **Aerial view of Bexhill 34** © Nathaniel, Adobe Stock
36. **Pevensey Bay 35** © Liliya Trott, Adobe Stock
37. **Aerial view of Pevensey Castle 36** © 2014 Barbara van Cleve – Wikimedia – Creative Commons Attribution-Share Alike 3.0 Unported license
38. **Archery Tavern c 1925 37** © Public Domain - Archery Tavern, Eastbourne autora National Brewery Heritage Trust - National Brewery Heritage Trust, United Kingdom - CC BY-SA. https://www.europeana.eu/hr/item/2059528/data_foodanddrink_658750   1920s
39. **Aerial photo of Sovereign harbour in Eastbourne along the entrance and the start of Pevensey bay. 38** © Geoff, Adobe Stock
40. **Eastbourne Pier and Bandstand 39** © Mark, Adobe Stock
41. **Aerial view of Eastbourne 41** © Alexey Fedorenko, Adobe Stock
42. **Eastbourne Redoubt 42** © 2014 Jenny Steel. Wikimedia - Creative Commons Attribution-Share Alike 3.0 Unported license
43. **Carpet Gardens, Grand Parade, Eastbourne 43** © Chris Brown, Adobe Stock
44. **Low tide at Beachy Head 44** © Melanie Hobson, Adobe Stock
45. **Beachy Head Lighthouse 45** © Makasana Photo, Adobe Stock
46. **Looking over Cuckmere Haven and the Seven Sisters white chalk cliffs 46** © pxlstore, Adobe Stock
47. **Belle Tout Lighthouse 47** © Kevin Eaves, Adobe Stock
48. **Aerial view of Belle Tout Lighthouse 49** © 2018 Mocsarbalaza. Wikimedia - Creative Commons Attribution-Share Alike 4.0 International license
49. **Seven Sisters and Birling Gap 50** © Rick Powell
50. **Tiger Inn, East Dean Green 51** © 2009 David Smith Wikimedia - Creative Commons Attribution 2.0 Generic license
51. **East Dean in Winter 50** © Oast House Archive, Wikimedia - Creative Commons Attribution-Share Alike

Richard Powell

52. *Friston Church 51* © farrington, Adobe Stock
53. *Friston Forest 53* © 2011 Mark Wordy, Flickr - Attribution 2.0 Generic (CC BY 2.0)
54. *Cuckmere River at Exceat 55* © 2019 DimiTalen, Creative Commons CC0 1.0 Universal Public Domain Dedication
55. *Pebble Beach, Seaford 57* © Bernd Brueggemann, Adobe Stock
56. *Seaford 58* © TADEUSZ IBROM, Adobe Stock
57. *Cliff House 59* © Public Domain (Copyright expired)
58. *Seaford Head 1906 59* © University of Sussex – Public Domain
59. *Seaford Head 60* © 2020 Tony Grist Poliphilo – Wikimedia - Creative Commons CC0 1.0 Universal Public Do-main Dedication
60. *Martello Tower Museum 61* © 2012 Dave Spicer. Wikimedia - Creative Commons Attribution-Share Alike 2.0 Generic license
61. *Remains of Tide Mills 62* © 2006 Tim Trent Wikimedia - Creative Commons Attribution-Share Alike 2.5 Generic license
62. *Newhaven Lighthouse 63* © 2013 Lee Roberts Wikimedia - Creative Commons Attribution-Share Alike 2.0 Generic license
63. *Looking at Newhaven beach from Fort Hill 64* © 陈阳/Wirestock Creators, Adobe Stock
64. *Newhaven Fort 65* © 2012 Paul Farmer Wikimedia - Creative Commons Attribution-Share Alike 2.0 Generic license
65. *Peacehaven Zero 66* © 2012 Stacey Harris Peacehaven – Geograph England and Ireland - Creative Commons Attribution-Share Alike 2.0 Generic license.
66. *Saltdean Lido 67* © 2010 Hassocks5489 Creative Commons CC0 1.0 Universal Public Domain Dedication
67. *Grand Ocean Hotel 68* © 2015 Lee Chatfield Creative Commons Attribution 2.0 Generic license.
68. *Rudyard Kipling's House 69* © Nicola, Adobe Stock
69. *Brighton Pavilion 70* © Alexey Fedorenko, Adobe Stock
70. *Brighton Marina 71* © 2011 Tanya Dedyukhina, Creative Commons Attribution 3.0 Unported
71. *French Convalescent Home 72* © 2013 Hassocks5489 Wikimedia - Creative Commons CC0 1.0 Universal Public Domain Dedication
72. *Lewes Crescent 74* © 2018 Hassocks5489 Wikimedia - Creative Commons CC0 1.0 Universal Public Domain Dedication
73. *Kemptown Brewery 75* © 2020 Ian Cunliffe. Geograph England and Ireland - Creative Commons Attribution-Share Alike 2.0 Generic license
74. *Brighton Chain Pier c.1890s 76* © Rijksmuseum Wikimedia - Creative Commons Zero, Public Domain Dedication
75. *The remains of Brighton West Pier, early morning 77* © 2018 Christerjet Wikimedia - Creative Commons Attribution 4.0 International license
76. *The remains of Brighton Palace Pier 77* © 2019 August Schwerdfeger Wikimedia - Creative Commons Attribution 4.0 International license
77. *Brighton Pavilion 78* © www.augustinflorian.ro, Adobe Stock
78. *Mazda Fountain 79* © Public Domain (Copyright expired)
79. *Angel of Peace 80* © 2009 Lee Chatfield Wikimedia - Creative Commons Attribution 2.0 Generic license. Flickr

80. *Palmeira Square, Hove 81* © Delia Suvari, Adobe Stock
81. *Palmeira Square 82* © 2013 Hassocks5489 Creative Commons CC0 1.0 Universal Public Domain Dedication
82. *Victorian Ironwork covered seating 83* © 2013 Hassocks5489 Creative Commons CC0 1.0 Universal Public Domain Dedication
83. *Hove Plinth 84* © Gill Copeland, Adobe Stock
84. *Hove Beach Huts 85* © Brian Scantlebury, Adobe Stock
85. *Old Shoreham 86* © Wikimedia – Public Domain - https://www.newberry.org/rights-and-reproductions
86. *Shoreham lifeboat station and lighthouse 87* © Jason Reid, Adobe Stock
87. *St Mary de Haura Church 87* © silvershadows, Adobe Stock
88. *Marlipins Museum 88* © 2014 Michael Coppins Wikimedia - Creative Commons Attribution-Share Alike 4.0 International license
89. *New Ferry Bridge 89* © 2017 Acabashi Creative Commons Attribution-ShareAlike 4.0 International licensing
90. *Shoreham Redoubt 90* © Nicola, Adobe Stock
91. *Lancing College Chapel 91* © 2014 Ian Cunliffe. Geograph - Creative Commons Attribution Share-alike license 2.0
92. *Looking towards Lancing College Chapel from Shoreham Footbridge 92* © Kenn, Adobe Stock
93. *Worthing Marine Gardens and Winchelsea Garden on the seafront 93* © Geoff, Adobe Stock
94. *Beach House Villa 94* © Pete Brant. This work has been released into the public domain by its author, at English Wikipedia. This applies worldwide
95. *Memorial for Warrior Birds 95* © 2009 The Voice of Hassocks the copyright holder of this work, releases this work into the public domain
96. *Worthing Pier 96* © 2011 Earldelawarr Wikimedia - Creative Commons Attribution-Share Alike 3.0 Unported license.
97. *Worthing Pier c.1900 96* © US Library of Congress ppmsc.09020 – Public Domain
98. *Pavilion Theatre 97* © 2018 The Wub. Wikimedia - Creative Commons Attribution-Share Alike 4.0 International license
99. *The Royal Arcade 98* © 2009 Miles Cary. Wikimedia - Creative Commons Attribution 2.0 Generic license.
100. *Worthing Seafront 99* © Alexey Fedorenko, Adobe Stock
101. *Sistine Ceiling at Goring 100* © 2012 Nick MacNeill. Wikimedia - Creative Commons Attribution-Share Alike 2.0 Generic license.
102. *Ferring Seafront 101* © Geoff, Adobe Stock
103. *Goring Gap, aerial view looking north of the West Sussex farming area between Goring and Ferring 102* © Geoff, Adobe Stock
104. *Rustington Convalescent home c1900 103* © Public Domain Detroit Publishing Co, 1890-1900
105. *Beach Huts 104* © 2010 Paul Gillett. Geograph - Creative Commons Attribution-Share Alike 2.0 Generic license.
106. *East Beach Café 105* © 2010 Thor. Wikimedia - Creative Commons Attribution 2.0 Generic license

107. *Longest Bench* 105 © 2015 Author, Richard Powell

108. *Littlehampton Harbour* 106 © 2015 Author, Richard Powell

109. *Coloured Houses Littlehampton* 106 © 2015 Author, Richard Powell

110. *Littlehampton Beach* 106 © 2015 Author, Richard Powell

111. *Oyster Pond c.1910* 107 © Public Domain (out of copyright)

112. *Littlehampton Harbour* 108 © 2015 Author, Richard Powell

113. *West Beach Littlehampton* 109 © 2015 Author, Richard Powell

114. *Littlehampton Fort* 109 © 2010 Kinnerton. Wikimedia - Creative Commons Attribution 3.0 Unported license

115. *Aerial view of Littlehampton* 110 © Alexey Fedorenko, Adobe Stock

116. *Felpham seafront* 111 © Nick Hawkes, Adobe Stock

117. *William Blake's Cottage* 112 © 2010 Colin Babb Geograph Creative Commons Attribution-Share Alike 2.0 Generic

118. *Felpham seafront* 113 © Geoff, Adobe Stock

119. *Butlin's Bognor* 114 © 2012 Stuart Jamieson Wikimedia - Creative Commons Attribution-Share Alike 2.0 Generic

120. *Bognor Pier* 115 © 2015 Mrs Ellacott Creative Commons Attribution-Share Alike 2.0 Generic

121. *Bognor Regis* 116 © Martin Valigursky, Adobe Stock

122. *Drinking Fountain* 118 © 2016 Jeff Gogarty. Geograph - Creative Commons Attribution-Share Alike 2.0 Generic

123. *Mulberry Harbour Wreckage* 119 © Wreck Group

124. *Aerial panorama of Chichester City Centre* 120 © 陈阳/Wirestock Creators, Adobe Stock

125. *A closer look at Chichester Cathedral* 121 © 2012 Evgeniy Podkopaev. Wikimedia - Creative Commons Attribution-Share Alike 3.0 Unported li-cense

126. *Sailboats and Saltmarsh* 122 © 2012 Colin Smith. Geograph - Creative Commons Attribution-Share Alike 2.0 Generic

127. *Dell Quay* 123 © Geoff, Adobe Stock

128. *Walkway at East Head* 124 © 2012 Shazz Geograph - Creative Commons Attribution-Share Alike 2.0 Generic

129. *Itchenor Village* 125 © 2013 Rob Farrow Geograph - Creative Commons Attribution-Share Alike 2.0 Generic

130. *Fishbourne Palace Model* 126 © 2007 Immanuel Giel, Wikimedia – Public Domain

131. *Fishbourne Palace Mosaic* 127 © 2013 Mattbuck Wikimedia - Creative Commons Attribution-Share Alike 2.0 Generic license.

132. *Bosham Harbour* 128 © 2014 Peter Trimming. Geograph - Creative Commons Attribution-Share Alike 2.0 Generic

133. *Bosham* 129 © Geoff, Adobe Stock

134. *Bosham* 130 © Woolcock Photo Library, Adobe Stock

135. *Seven Sisters* 131 © 2015 Colin & Linda McKie